He's Put The Whole World In Her Hands.

Imprimatur:

+Donald E. Pelotte
s.s.s.

Bishop of Gallup

Published
by
Roman, Inc.
555 Lawrence Avenue, Roselle, Illinois 60172

ISBN 0-937739-09-X

Second printing, 1990, USA

Compiled and edited
by
Dan Paulos

Quotations of Mother Teresa of Calcutta, India

Used by permission of Mother Teresa and her Missionaries of Charity.

Calligraphy
by
Dan Paulos and Friends:

Anne Batten
Elke Belcher
Ken Brown
Michelle Calaba
Pat Crawford
Molly Gaylor
Helen Gershen
Hiroko Gibney
Sally Jones
Pamela La Regina
Donna Lee
Sarah Logan

Dege Cole-Lowry
Megan Lucas
JoEllen Moline
Eda Mosely
Jerilynne Nibbe
Vivian Olson
Syed Pervaiz
Jean Marie Seaton
Elise Steele
Martha Link-Walsh
Andrée Weinman

Special thanks to the Society for Calligraphy.

To Sister Mary Jean Dorcy, O.P.
who taught me to cut

To Sister DeLourdes Bragg, S.C.C.
who taught me calligraphy

To my mother and father
who taught me to love

And to Mother Teresa, M.C.
who brought it all together

FOREWORD

Little did I know when I received that first letter from Dan about eighteen years ago, that this young man in his early twenties would become what seems to me now, more spirit and artistry than flesh and blood.

One of eight children, Dan was born to a hard working family in Sioux City, Iowa. Early in his life he learned to love the ways and the world of the Catholic Church, its music, meditation, the chanting and prayers, above all, the living spirit of the Holy Trinity.

He began to show his devotion to the Church when he learned to play the piano. He loved playing for the nuns in the near-by convent. He also played the organ with the same fervor and reverence. When only fourteen he became director of an adult choir.

Even as a child he knew that he did not fit into many categories; and school for him was a total waste of time. He was a very poor student. He preferred doing chores and running errands for the elderly. Upon completing his third year in high school, he left home to join the religious Order of the Brothers of the Good Shepherd, dedicated to caring for the underprivileged. After struggling for nearly a decade with religious politics, he decided to leave the Order.

Early on he was shown the paper-cuttings of Sister Mary Jean Dorcy, world renowned for her religious cut-outs. With the same spiritual excitement, he started painting sacred pictures.

Dan must have known that this would be his way of portraying his ardor and devotion to his church.

Although he bloodied his fingers when he first started to cut his delicate pictures with a double edge razor blade, later cutting with scissors and honed razor would be his technique.

His respect for his teacher was evident to the end of her life. Sister Dorcy wrote of Dan: "He deeply admired my black and white cut-outs, which he studied for years. He asked me for help in black and white work, which I readily gave. He studied my use of chiaroscuro and the spiritual meaning of the pictures, and out of this emerged a style completely his own. Where my cuttings have a fanciful lightness of touch, Dan's are strong and forceful, taking on a free and independent form. It is said that the differences between our works are greater than the similarities. I am so proud of Dan, even though I really have no right to be. It is *his* talent and *his* expertise. But as my student, yes, he has made me very proud, because what it took me thirty years to accomplish, he achieved in two."

Dan's concern for suffering humans is found in the fine lines of his silhouettes — delicate as silk thread. It seems to me that there's a prayer in each one. I think if he drew and cut little black rain drops all over a white paper, they'd sparkle radiate, glorious white halos appearing around each one, so close to his spirit is each picture.

With all Dan's devotion to the serious and soulful beauty of the Holy Family, he remembers to balance his artistic works with an occasional touch of humor.

His first book, SPRING COMES TO THE HILL COUNTRY, was a collaboration with his mentor and friend Sister Dorcy. He organized and lettered the manuscript which contains 52 of Sister's precious cuttings.

Dan sent a copy to Mother Teresa of Calcutta, suggesting that if she liked the book, they collaborate on the next volume. Mother agreed. And for three years he has worked steadily on completing HE'S PUT THE WHOLE WORLD IN HER HANDS.

To Dan, Mother Teresa is a living saint. Was it great good-fortune then or the spirit of God Himself that brought her together with Dan to produce these pages? Her quotations and Dan's cuttings are separate entities, but the undercurrent flows from the same Source and I must believe that God has guided them through the making of this extraordinary book.

Joan Baez, Sr.
Palo Alto, CA

Paper-cuttings
by
Dan Paulos

Unity among Christians is important
because we represent a light for others.
If we are Christians, we must resemble Christ.
I believe this very deeply. Gandhi once said that
if Christians lived their faith completely, there
would be no Hindus left in India. People expect us
to live our Christianity fully.

From Our Lady we must ask
for a delicate love for the poor.

since You are Jesus in His suffering,
deign also to be to me a patient Jesus,
overlooking my faults, seeing only my
intentions, which are to love
You and serve You in the person of each of Your chil-
dren who suffer.

O, LORD,
INCREASE
MY FAITH.

Maintain the silence
    that Jesus maintained
    for those thirty years
    at Nazareth,
    and that He still maintains
    in the tabernacle,
    interceding for us.
    Pray like the Virgin Mary,
    who kept all things
    quietly in her heart
    through prayer
    and meditation,
    and still does,
    as mediatrix of all graces.

I am only a small instrument in God's hand.

Our Lord and Our Lady

gave all the glory to God the Father;

like them, in a very, very small way,

I also want to give all glory

to the Father.

We must love her as he loved her! To be a cause of joy as he was. Staying close to her as he kept. Sharing with her everything, even the cross.

Jesus came to reveal the Father.

In the time of the
Old Testament.
God was known as
the God of fear,
punishment, and anger.

The coming of Jesus
reverses this picture completely.

Mary
can teach us
silence
and how to keep
all things
in our
hearts.

All of us are but
His instruments,
who do our little bit
and pass by

Love to pray.

FEEL OFTEN THE NEED TO PRAY. AND TAKE THE TROUBLE TO PRAY! IT IS BY PRAYING OF TEN THAT WE WILL PRAY BETTER. PRAYER ENLARGES THE HEART UNTIL IT IS CAPABLE OF CONTAI- NING THE GIFT THAT GOD MAKES OF HIMSELF. ASK AND SEEK: YOUR HEART WILL GROW CAPABLE OF RECEIVING HIM AND HOLDING ON TO HIM. LOVE TO PRAY.

BEFORE ALMIGHTY GOD...

we are all poor.

Receive the symbol of your crucified Lord.
Follow His footsteps in search of souls.
Spread the charity of His heart wherever you go
especially to the ones most in need.
Carry Him and His light into the homes of the poor,
and so satiate His thirst for souls.

There
must be a reason
why some people can
afford to live so well. They
must have worked for it.
I only feel angry when I
see waste. When I see
people throwing away
things that we could
USE

Do not wait
        for leaders.
Do it all alone;
person to person.

Our Lord on the cross possessed nothing.
He was on the cross which was given by Pilate.
The nails and the crown were given by the soldiers.
He was naked, and when He died ... cross, nails,
and crown were taken away from Him,
and He was wrapped in a shroud given Him
by a kind heart, and buried in a tomb
which, also, was not His.

There should be less talk;
a preaching point is not
a meeting point.

What do you do, then?

Take a broom and clean
someone's house.
That will say enough!

And so
in Christ
it was proved
that the greatest
gift is love:
because
through His
suffering He paid
for our sins.

WITHOUT
MARY
THERE IS NO
JESUS.

God
is
the friend
of silence.
WE NEED TO FIND GOD,
but
we
cannot
find Him
in
noise
or in
excitement.

How much we can learn from Our Lady!
She was so humble because she was all for God.
She was full of grace.
Tell Our Lady to tell Jesus:
"They have no wine; they need the wine of
humility and meekness; of kindness and sweetness."

She is sure to tell us,
"Do whatever He tells you."

LOVELY LADY DRESSED IN BLUE

TEACH ME HOW TO PRAY;

CHRIST WAS ONCE A LITTLE BOY

TELL ME WHAT TO SAY.

IF WE REALLY
WANT TO
———— PRAY
WE MUST FIRST
LEARN TO
———— LISTEN,
FOR IN THE SILENCE
OF THE HEART
———— GOD SPEAKS.

Jesus has chosen us for Himself.
We belong to Him.
Let us be so convinced
of this "BELONGING"
that we allow nothing,
however small,
to separate us from His love.

The most beautiful part of Our Lady was that when Jesus came into her life, immediately, in haste, she went to St. Elizabeth's place to give Jesus to her and to her son. And we read in the Gospel that the child "Leapt with Joy" at this first contact with the Savior.

If you are a saint,

Thank God!

When we look
at His cross·
we understand
His love ✣ His
head is bent
down to kiss
us ✣ His hands
are extended to
embrace us ✣
His heart is
wide open
to receive
us——·

WHAT IS HAPPENING TODAY ON THE SURFACE OF THE CHURCH WILL PASS. **FOR CHRIST, THE CHURCH IS THE SAME TODAY, YESTER DAY, TOMORROW. ✝** THE APOSTLES WENT THROUGH THE SAME FEELINGS OF FEAR AND DISTRUST, FAILURE AND DISLOYALTY, AND YET CHRIST DID NOT SCOLD THEM +++ JUST "LITTLE CHILDREN, LITTLE FAITH, WHY DID YOU FEAR?" I WISH WE COULD LOVE AS HE DID— NOW!

The Magnificat

is Our Lady's prayer of thanks.

She can help us to love Jesus best;
she is the one who can show us
the shortest way
to Him.

Let us go to her with great love and trust.

Be kind and merciful!
Let no one ever come
to you without leaving
better and happier.

OUR LORD

AT HIS DYING MOMENT,
THOUGHT OF HIS MOTHER. xxx: THAT
IS THE PROOF THAT HE WAS HUMAN
TO THE LAST. xxxxxxx: THEREFORE,
IF YOU HAVE A LOVING NATURE,
AND A SMILING TEMPERAMENT,
KEEP IT AND USE IT

FOR

GOD

I think
if Jesus was able
to listen to
Our Lady, we, too
should be able
to listen to Him.

At the foot of the
cross we find her,
sharing with Christ
in his passion;

Again and again
she comes into
our lives, into the
life of the world, to
bring joy and peace.

To lead us back to God.

We need to trust
our poor people.
The greatest injustice
done to our poor is
that we fail to trust
them, to love them.
How often we just
push and pull.

A living love hurts.
Jesus, to prove His love,
died on the cross for us.
The mother,
to give birth to her child,
has to suffer.
If you really love one another
properly,
there must be great sacrifice.

CHRIST
CAME INTO THE WORLD
TO PUT CHARITY
IN ITS PROPER PERSPECTIVE.

LET JESUS USE YOU
WITHOUT CONSULTATION!

Make me, O Lord,
appreciative of the dignity of my high
vocation, and it's many responsibilities.
Never permit me to disgrace it by
giving way to coldness,
unkindness, or
impatience.

People
throughout the world
may look different or
have a different religion· edu
cation or position· but they are
all the same· They are all people
to be loved· They are all hungry for
love· The people you see in the streets
of India or Hong Kong are hung
ry in body· but the people in
London or New York have
also a hunger which must
be satisfied· Every
person needs to
be loved·

She has given us

JESUS

By joyously becoming
His mother,
She became the
Mediatress
in the salvation
of mankind.

Many years ago an angel came to bring the good news to Mary. The Prince of Peace was anxious to come to earth and an angel was used to bring the good news that the Creator would become a little child. The Prince of Peace was attracted to a young girl, who was a nobody in the eyes of the world. Even the angel could not understand why he was sent to a creature like that. But she was so beautiful that the King of kings wanted to become flesh in her. She was so full of grace, so pure, so full of God. She looked at the angel ... she must have been surprised for she had never seen an angel... and asked, how? What are you saying? I don't understand; it makes no sense to me. And the angel said simply that by the power of the Holy Spirit, Christ would be formed within her. And Mary answered with just one word:

"Behold the handmaid of the lord."

i am
but the
pencil
in the hand
of God

Put your heart into being a bright Light.

The first Christians died for Jesus.
They were recognized
because
they loved one another.

The world
has NEVER needed more love
than today.

Everybody seems to be in such a terrible rush today, anxious for greater developments and greater riches - so that our children have very little time with their parents. ~ Parents have little time for each other, and in the home begins the disruption of the

PEACE of the WORLD.

Make certain that you let God's grace
work in your souls by accepting
whatever He gives you, and giving
whatever He takes from you.

True holiness consists in doing
God's will with a smile.

Salve, Regina, mater mi-se-ricordiae: Vita, dulce-
do, et spes no-   s, exsules, fi-
li-i hev   s in hac
lacrime   os tuos
miseric   benedi-
ctu   en-
de. O clemens: O piar: O dulcis Virgo Maria.

AT THE FOOT OF THE CROSS
SHE BECAME OUR MOTHER ALSO,
BECAUSE JESUS SAID
WHEN HE WAS DYING,
THAT HE GAVE
HIS MOTHER
TO ST. JOHN,
AND ST. JOHN
TO HIS MOTHER.
AT THAT VERY MOMENT
WE BECAME HER CHILDREN.

LET US PRAY

that we shall be able to welcome
Jesus at Christmas not in the
cold manger of our heart, but in a
heart full of love and humility, a
heart warm

WITH LOVE
FOR ONE
ANOTHER

The work is God's work.
The poor are God's poor.

Put yourself completely under the influence
of Jesus
so that He may
think His thoughts in your mind,
do His work through your hands;

for you will be all powerful
with Him to strengthen you.

PUT YOUR SINS IN THE CHALICE
FOR THE SACRED BLOOD TO WASH AWAY.

IS CAPABLE OF WASHING AWAY
ALL THE SINS OF THE WORLD.

St. Teresa of Avila ? Oh no! I haven't called myself after the big Teresa, but after the little one, Teresa of Lisieux.

JESUS, MY SUFFERING LORD,

grant that today
and every day I may
see You in the person
of Your sick ones,
and that caring for them
I may see You.
Grant also that even in the
guise of the fretful, the
demanding, the unreasonable
I may still recognize
You and say: "My
suffering Jesus

HOW SWEET IT IS TO SERVE YOU.

Today, once again, when Jesus comes
amongst His own
His own don't know Him!

He comes in the rotten bodies of our poor:
He comes even in the rich, choked by their own riches.
He comes in the loneliness of their hearts,
and when there is no one to love them.

Jesus comes to you and to me
and often very, very often
We pass Him by.

A Christian
is a
tabernacle
of the living
God.

Mother
Mary
is
the
hope
of
mankind.

I try to give to the poor
people for love what the
rich could get for money.
No, I wouldn't touch a
leper for a thousand pounds;
yet I willingly cure him
for the Love of God.

KEEP THE *Light of Christ*
ALWAYS BURNING IN YOUR HEART —
FOR HE ALONE IS THE WAY TO WALK.
HE IS THE LIFE TO LIVE.
HE IS THE LOVE TO LOVE.

He's Put The
Whole World
In Her Hands.

In heaven everything was beautiful—yet, what attracted Jesus to Earth? The Son of God wanted to feel what it meant to be a human being; to be locked up for nine months, so dependent on a mother. That is why we say "He, being rich, became poor, so helpless!

Let us all stop using

GUNS and BOMBS

to overcome the world.

Let us use love and compassion. Peace begins

with a smile ~ ~ smile five times a day at

someone you don't really want to smile at ~

do it for peace. So let

us radiate the peace of

God and so light His

light, extinguishing in

the hearts of all men,

all hatred ~ and love

for power.

Let us not be satisfied
with just giving money;
money is not enough.

The poor need our hands
to serve them. They need
our hearts to love them.

We must make our homes
centers
of compassion -
- and forgive endlessly.

WE
MUST
ALL
LEARN
TO LOVE
WITHOUT
DISCRIMINATION.

Our words are useless
unless they come
from the bottom of the heart.
Words that do not give
the light of Christ
only make
the darkness worse.

THIS INDEX DEFINES THE PAGE NUMBERS, TITLES AND SIZES OF THE CUTTINGS, THE YEAR COMPLETED, OWNERS OF THE ORIGINALS, AND THE CALLIGRAPHERS — IN CAPITAL LETTERS.

Page 107
BRIGHT STAR OF DAVID
12 by 21
1987
Jerry and Lucille Hochwender
Sioux City, Iowa
DAN PAULOS, Albuquerque, NM

Page 110
THE GOOD SHEPHERD
12 by 16 1/2
1988
John and Sylvia Teem
Arlington, VA
KEN BROWN, Hugo OK

Page 112
O TOWERING PILLARS OF FREEDOM!
19 inches
1986
John Albright
District Heights, MD
ELKE BELCHER, Corona del Mar, CA

Page 113
OUR LADY, QUEEN OF PEACE
14 by 19 1/2
1987
Mary Cacace
Yonkers, NY
DAN PAULOS, Albuquerque, NM

Page 115
MUSIC MADONNA
13 1/2 by 15
1985
Joseph W. Bean
San Francisco, CA
MICHELLE CALABA, Newbury Park, CA

Page 118
OUR LADY OF THE VIETNAM VETERANS
19 1/2 by 22 1/2
1989
DAN PAULOS, Albuquerque, NM

Page 120
THE SWEETEST GIFT, A MOTHER'S SMILE
9 1/2 by 11 1/2
1986
Jo Ann Toepfer
Albuquerque, NM
ELISE STEELE, Santa Barbara, CA

Page 122
BEHOLD OUR KING!
13 by 20
1987
DAN PAULOS, Albuquerque, NM

Page 124
HE LOVES WITHOUT DISCRIMINATION
10 by 17 1/2
1987
DAN PAULOS, Albuquerque, NM

Page 126
MARY'S LAST AUTUMN
12 by 16
1986
Jeannette Paulos (artist's grandmother)
Sioux City, Iowa
EVA MOSELY, Santa Barbara, CA